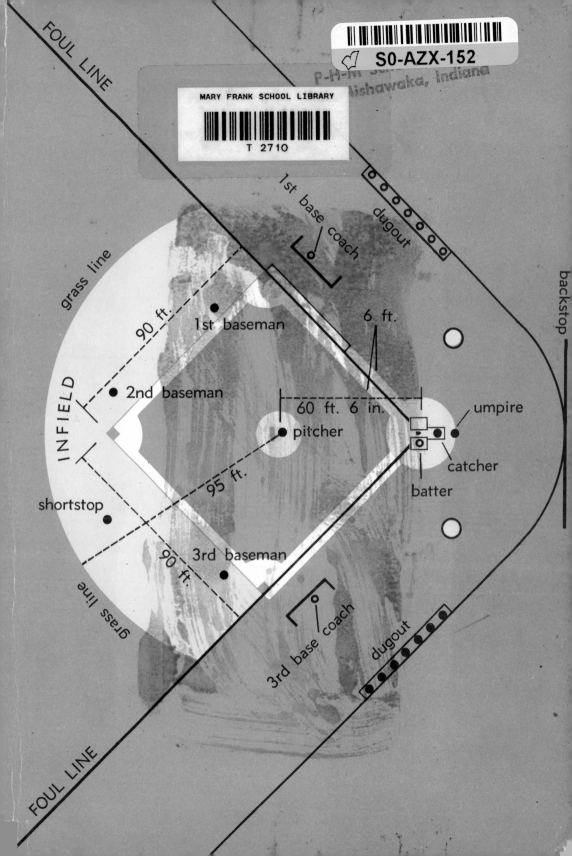

FOUL LINE

1st base coach

dugout

backstop

grass line

90 ft.

1st baseman

6 ft.

INFIELD

2nd baseman

60 ft. 6 in.

umpire

pitcher

catcher

95 ft.

batter

shortstop

90 ft.

3rd baseman

grass line

3rd base coach

dugout

FOUL LINE

HENRY AARON

HOME-RUN KING

★ ★ ★ ★ ★ ★ ★ ★ ★ ★

BY SAM AND BERYL EPSTEIN

GARRARD PUBLISHING COMPANY
CHAMPAIGN, ILLINOIS

Sports Consultant:

COLONEL RED REEDER

Former Member of the West Point Coaching Staff
and Special Assistant to the West Point
Director of Athletics

Library of Congress Cataloging in Publication Data

Epstein, Samuel, 1909–
    Henry Aaron, home-run king.

    1. Aaron, Henry, 1934–   —Juvenile liter-
ature. 2. Baseball—Juvenile literature. I. Ep-
stein, Beryl Williams, 1910–   joint author.
II. Title.
GV865.A25E67   796.357'092'4 [B]   75-9966
ISBN 0-8116-6674-3

Photo credits:

The Braves, Atlanta, Georgia: p. 23
Indianapolis Recorder: p. 20
Wide World: pp. 8, 60 (top), 71 (top), jacket
United Press International: pp. 1, 3, 4, 13, 27, 30, 37, 40, 45, 48 (both),
    53, 56, 60 (middle and bottom) 65, 71 (bottom), 76,
    85 (all), 92, 95

Contents

Opening day, 1974. It's Aaron's first time up, his first swing at the ball, and home run number 714 is on its way!

1. "He Did It!"

April 4, 1974, opening day of the major-league baseball season, was bright and sunny in Cincinnati. A record-breaking crowd filled Riverfront Stadium as the Atlanta Braves and the Cincinnati Reds trotted out onto the diamond.

At exactly 2:30 P.M. United States Vice-President Gerald Ford threw out the first ball. Then Jack Billingham, the Reds' pitcher, hurled the first pitch. Six minutes later the Braves had men on first and second, and one out.

Suddenly the stands burst into wild cheering. Henry Aaron, Number 44, had moved up to the plate.

An umpire hurried out to the mound to give Billingham a new ball.

Aaron propped his bat against his leg, its butt on the ground. It was his usual 34-ounce, 34½-inch bat. He put on his batting helmet, carefully settling it with both hands. Then, looking at Billingham over his left shoulder, he picked up the bat and cocked it high.

The cheering of the fans died away to a solemn hush.

Billingham reared back and threw. The pitch was low.

"Ball!" came the umpire's call.

Billingham's second pitch was a slow curve that missed the plate for ball two.

The third pitch was a fast ball over the outside corner.

"Strike!" the umpire announced.

The fourth pitch was a low outside sinker.

"Ball three!"

Billingham took a deep breath. Then his fifth pitch sped to the plate.

Henry Aaron watched it coming. At the last possible moment, his arms and body swung. His powerful wrists whipped the bat forward. Wood cracked against leather. The ball sailed away in a low, flat arc.

The crowd rose to its feet as Henry Aaron started down the base line. All eyes, except his, were following the ball. It flew over left center field. It traveled 200 feet . . . 300 feet. . . .

The ball was heading for the twelve-foot fence—a brown fence with a yellow stripe along its top. At the foot of the fence, 400 feet from home plate, a Reds' fielder waited. His gloved hand was high, ready for a rebound.

And then the ball topped that yellow stripe by three feet and disappeared!

A mighty, ear-splitting roar rose from the stands.

Thousands of happy fans shouted and screamed. Feet stamped. Banners waved. "He did it! He did it!"

Nobody had to look at the figures flashing on the scoreboard. Everyone knew that Henry Aaron had just hit his 714th home run. Everyone knew that that run tied what had been called "the greatest record in all of sports"—the lifetime home-run record of baseball's most famous slugger, Babe Ruth.

Aaron is all smiles after tying the lifetime home-run record of Babe Ruth.

Even faithful Cincinnati fans were joining in the celebration. For that moment Henry Aaron of the Braves was, as one sportswriter said, their "beloved enemy." He had given them a memory that would never fade. They had watched him make baseball history.

Henry's grinning teammates were waiting for him. Some of the men had tears of joy and pride in their eyes.

Grinning himself now, head high, Henry Aaron crossed home plate.

And when the Reds' manager talked about it later, he expressed the thought that millions of people shared that day. He said, "It couldn't have happened to a better man, a finer gentleman."

2. Growing Up in Mobile

When Henry Aaron was a small boy, he was very shy. Usually he played by himself in his own backyard.

He had a ball made of rags tied together with string. He threw it into the air and tried to catch it when it came down.

He also had a little rubber ball that he could throw onto the roof of his house. When it rolled off, he batted it against the wall with a broom handle. He always held his homemade bat cross-handed.

Herbert Aaron, Henry's father, had once

played good semi-professional baseball. But now Mr. Aaron worked long hours in a shipyard to make enough money to feed his large family. There were two children older than Henry, who was born February 5, 1934. There were also five younger ones. They crowded every inch of space in the Aarons' small house in Mobile, Alabama.

Henry was about twelve years old when his father said, "Why don't you go over to the park and see Mr. Jackson, son? I hear he's set up a boys' softball league."

So Henry joined a team that played other softball teams all over Mobile.

When he wasn't playing, he spent most of his spare time reading about real baseball and listening to games over the radio. The year he was thirteen, he read everything he could find about Jackie Robinson of the Dodgers. Robinson had just become the first black player in the major leagues. This made him a special hero to black boys like Henry Aaron.

"Come on, Henry," Mr. Aaron said one day that summer. "The Dodgers are in town, and you and I are going to see them."

Henry watched Jackie Robinson all during the game.

"I'm going to be like him someday," he told his father.

"Maybe, son." His father smiled. "But first you're going to get an education."

Henry's high school had no baseball team, but he played football there. College scouts said, "This boy is so good that he could get a football scholarship." But Henry decided football might injure his throwing arm, so he quit after a year.

One day Henry was playing hookey from school. Mr. Aaron walked past a pool hall and saw Henry inside.

Jackie Robinson, first black player in the
major leagues, was Henry's hero.

A moment later Mr. Aaron had Henry
by the arm. "What are you doing here?"
he demanded.

Henry pointed to a radio. "I'm listening
to a Dodger game," he said.

"You're coming home with me now," his
father told him.

For two hours they talked together in
the old car that was parked in their
yard.

"But if I'm planning to be a baseball

player," Henry said, "I can learn more by listening to a game than I can in school."

"Look, son," his father said. "I had to leave school to earn money. I'm working hard just so you won't have to do that. You're going to finish high school and go on to college."

Henry knew the argument was over. From then on he went to school every day. But he still played ball whenever he could, except on Sundays. His mother didn't approve of Sunday games.

He held down third base in a softball game one afternoon. Afterward a man named Ed Scott came over to see him. Henry had often seen Scott before. He was a scout for the Black Bears, Mobile's fastest semi-pro team.

"How would you like to play with the Black Bears on Sundays?" Scott asked.

"The Black Bears!" Henry said. Then he

remembered. "Mama won't let me play on Sundays," he said.

But Scott didn't give up. He went to the Aaron house and talked to Henry's mother. "It's a great opportunity for a fifteen-year-old kid," he told her.

"Please, mama!" Henry begged.

Finally Mrs. Aaron gave in.

It was a big day for Henry when he began to play real baseball with grown men. Usually he was the Bears' short-stop, but he played other positions too. He still batted cross-handed.

After every game the Bears' owner gave each player a few dollars. When Henry got ten dollars one day, he could scarcely believe it. He had often earned 25 or 50 cents mowing lawns. He had never had ten dollars all at once before.

Late in the summer of 1951 the Bears played an important game. It was with the Indianapolis Clowns of the Negro

American League. A big crowd turned out to watch Mobile's hometown Bears meet these real professionals.

Seventeen-year-old Henry hit a double and two singles that day. He did some good fielding too.

Afterward a Clowns official took him aside. "Would you like to play for us for $200 a month?" the man asked.

Henry was sure the man was just kidding him. "Why not?" he said.

"When do you get out of school?" the man asked.

"I'll graduate next year," Henry told him.

"Then I'll send you a contract next spring," the man said.

Henry still didn't believe him. But someday, he promised himself, he would get an offer like that from someone who really meant it.

One October day that year he was hurrying home from school. The Dodgers and the Giants were in a play-off for the National League pennant. That afternoon's game would decide the winner. He wanted to be in time to hear the end of it over the radio.

The sound of the broadcast came through the open door of a house that he was passing. He stopped to listen. It was the bottom of the ninth and the Dodgers were winning, 4-2. The Giants' Bobby Thomson was at bat, with two men on base. Henry heard the crack of wood. Then he heard cheering. Thomson had homered—and given the Giants a victory with a score of 5-4!

Thomson must be the proudest man in the world, Henry thought, and suddenly he started to run. He ran all the way home, with his head high in the air. He was pretending to be Bobby Thomson, heading for the plate with the cheers of the crowd in his ears.

3. A Contract!

Early the next year a Clowns contract arrived at the Aaron house by mail. The letter with it told Henry to report for spring training.

It wasn't easy to persuade Henry's parents to let him go. His mother cried when the whole family took him to the train on the day he left. But she gave him two dollars and some sandwiches in a paper bag.

Henry had never been away from home before. He waved as the train moved off and wondered if maybe he had made a mistake after all.

He was scared when he arrived at the Clowns' chilly camp in Winston-Salem, North Carolina. The manager passed out warm-up jackets to most of the players. Henry didn't get one.

Other players took their turns in the batting cage. Henry got in for only a few swings.

But Syd Pollock, the Clowns' owner, was watching him.

"How can he do so well when he bats cross-handed?" Pollock said. He told the trainer to teach Henry the right way to hit.

Henry didn't enjoy the next weeks. He didn't like having to learn a new way of holding the bat. He was spending most of his time on the bench. The regular members of the team didn't talk to him.

Once the second baseman looked at him and said, "It won't be long now before we get rid of some of these green kids."

On the Clowns' old bus, traveling from town to town, Henry usually slept. When he was asleep he could forget for a while how lonely and miserable he was.

The first time he got into the line-up was the day of a doubleheader against the powerful Kansas City Monarchs. In the first game that day he hit a home run, a single, and two doubles. In the second game he got six hits.

Suddenly everything changed. Henry be-

The Indianapolis Clowns were still going strong ten years after Aaron's move to the major leagues.

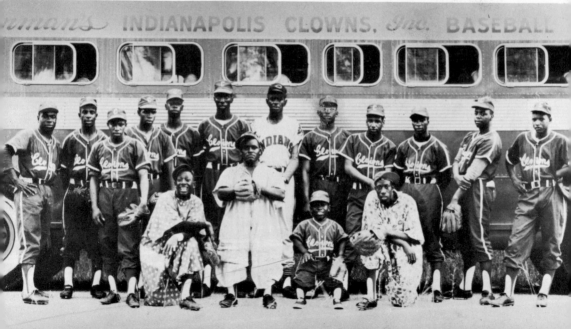

came the team's regular shortstop. The other players realized he could help them win games. They began to talk to him. "He's a good kid," they decided. They called him Little Brother.

Henry's average climbed to a dizzy .467. He heard that major-league scouts were sending in reports on him.

Six weeks after he had joined the Clowns, Pollock called him into his office.

"I've had two offers for you, Henry," Pollock said. "The New York Giants will pay you $250 a month and send you to one of their Class A teams. The Braves will pay you $300 a month and send you to a Class C club. Which do you want?"

Henry looked calm. But inside he was very excited and scared. Leaving the Clowns now would be like leaving home all over again. But he knew that if he ever hoped to be like Jackie Robinson, he had to take this chance.

Was he ready for the Giants' Class A club? he asked himself. He thought he could learn more on a Class C team. And, besides, the Braves were offering him more money. His family could use every dollar he sent them.

"I'll go with the Braves," Henry said.

He didn't receive a bonus for signing up. He didn't even know he might have asked for one. He thanked Syd Pollock for the cheap paper suitcase the Clowns gave him as a farewell gift. Pollock, he learned later, had sold Henry's contract for $10,000.

"You'll play with our Northern League team in Eau Claire, Wisconsin," a Braves scout told Henry. Then he handed him a plane ticket to Eau Claire.

Henry had never been on an airplane. He was shaking with fright the day he climbed aboard. He was still shaking when the plane landed.

New man on the team Henry Aaron signs
autographs for Eau Claire's young fans.

Now once more the older players ignored their new shortstop. And now the
other players were white. Henry had never
played with white players before.

After about two weeks he felt so lonely
he telephoned his family. He told them
he was coming home. His brother talked
him out of it.

The next day the team manager said,
"You'll be playing on the All-Star team,
Henry. You've been voted the league's All-
Star shortstop."

23

After that things were better. Now Henry felt he really belonged to the team. He made friends with two other black teammates, and they all roomed together at the YMCA. He discovered that the white townspeople were friendly. His hitting got better and better.

At the end of the season, his batting average of .336 was the second highest in the league. He was named the league's Rookie of the Year.

"I've got some good news for you, Henry," the manager told him. "You're going into spring training next year with the Milwaukee Braves' Triple A team."

From Class C to Triple A in one year wasn't too bad, Henry told himself as he headed for home. For the first time since he had left Mobile, he felt sure he could become a real ballplayer. Henry thought even his parents would agree about that now.

4. A Good Manager

Henry Aaron felt fine when he reported for spring training in Florida the next season. He felt even better after slamming out two home runs.

Then he learned that the team's manager didn't think much of him. "He'll never be good enough for the major leagues," the manager had said. "He can't hit to the right."

Henry's heart sank. He was sure the manager was even sorry Henry had been brought up to his Triple A team.

So Henry went to see the big boss— the farm-team director. "Send me back down," he begged.

The director had watched Henry and thought he was doing pretty well. But he also knew how the team's manager felt. He decided Henry would do better under another manager.

"I'll send you to the Braves' farm camp at Waycross, Georgia," he said. "Maybe somebody there can use you."

"I'll go anyplace," Henry said.

The Waycross camp was a field and a rough barracks in a pine forest. The one good thing about it, Henry thought, was a Class A team manager named Ben Geraghty.

"He was a good manager, the best I ever played for," Henry wrote years later in a book about his life in baseball.

Geraghty decided right away that he wanted Henry as second baseman on his Jacksonville, Florida, team in the Class A South Atlantic, or Sally, League. Only one thing worried Geraghty. The other

Promising new hitter Henry Aaron gets a few words of advice from Ben Geraghty.

Sally League players were all white, and the team played only in the South. And in those days, in the South, blacks and whites couldn't stay at the same hotels.

"You'd be the first black player in the league," he told Henry. "It wouldn't be easy, son."

"I grew up in the South," Henry said. "I know what it's like."

"All right," Geraghty said. "Then I'll take you." Later he decided to take along another black player too.

27

Henry liked Jacksonville from the start. He met pretty Barbara Lucas, a student in business college. Her family made him feel at home in their house. They kept him from missing his own family very much.

He wasn't upset because he couldn't stay with the white members of the team or eat with them. But he did mind when white fans booed him and his team's new black center fielder. He made up his mind to be so good that the fans would forget his color.

His batting average moved up to .362. Even when he slumped, he was sure the slump wouldn't last. It never did.

Once he went hitless for a few days. Joe Andrews, a teammate, teased Henry about it.

"What are you doing to pull out of this slump?" Joe asked.

Henry decided to kid Joe along.

"Oh, I called Stan Musial about it," he said. Musial, one of baseball's great hitters, was then at the peak of his career.

Joe believed Henry. He was sure that Henry was much too shy and quiet to kid anybody. "You called Musial!" he said. "What did he tell you?"

"Oh, he just told me to keep swinging," Henry said.

That night he got two doubles. And Joe told everyone what Henry had said. A few days later a newspaper headline announced: Stan Musial Helps Jacksonville Rookie!

Another sportswriter asked Henry about the story. Henry grinned and told him the truth.

Henry made mistakes at second base. But Geraghty always told him what he had done wrong and how to correct it.

That season Henry made 208 hits, including 36 doubles. He scored 115 runs and drove in another 125. Nineteen-year-old Henry Aaron was named the league's Most Valuable Player.

The men in the Braves' head office decided Henry's hitting was major-league quality. But they weren't as happy with his work at second base. They felt he still had a lot to learn there.

"Maybe he'd come up faster as an outfielder," someone said. "Why don't we get him winter training in the outfield?"

In 1953 Henry Aaron was named the Most Valuable Player of the Sally League.

The Braves' farm director telephoned Henry. "Would you be willing to play in Puerto Rico this winter?" he asked.

"Sounds all right to me," Henry said.

Henry and Barbara were married on October 6, and the young newlyweds spent their honeymoon in Puerto Rico. Henry played ball there all winter.

By spring he still wasn't an expert out-fielder. He was assigned to Toledo, the Braves' top Triple A club. But he was hitting so well that the Braves wanted to keep an eye on him. They sent him to train at their own major-league camp.

The Braves had finished in second place the year before. That had been their first season in Milwaukee. They had moved there from Boston. The Milwaukee fans were proud to have their own major-league team. They had made heroes of the players, and the players wanted to win a pennant for them.

Over the winter the team had added more power with some good trades. The most important trade was for a new left fielder, Bobby Thomson. Henry could remember listening to the radio the day Thomson's homer won the 1951 pennant for the Giants. He knew that the Braves counted on Thomson to help lead them to a victory too.

Henry worked hard that spring of 1954. During a few exhibition games the Braves used him as a pinch hitter. One tremendous homer Henry banged out for them landed outside the Sarasota stadium.

"That may be the longest home run anyone will ever hit in this park," someone said.

On March 13, at St. Petersburg, the Braves played the New York Yankees. Henry saw Thomson hit a double, tear around first, and slide into second. Then he saw Thomson lie there, with his leg doubled under him. The Braves' star had to be carried off the field.

Henry wondered what would happen if Thomson were badly hurt. He thought there were two or three men in line to replace him.

The next morning he learned that a broken ankle would keep Thomson out of the line-up for weeks. All the Braves looked unhappy as they got ready to play the Cincinnati Reds.

Perhaps Charlie Grimm, the Braves' manager, remembered Henry's tremendous home run in Sarasota. Anyhow, he suddenly picked up Henry's glove and tossed it to him.

"You're my left fielder, kid," he said. "The job's yours until somebody takes it away from you."

5. Rookie with the Braves

That afternoon Henry hit the Boston Red Sox for a single, a triple, and a homer. The next day he got a single and a triple against the Yankees. His average for the Braves' spring exhibition games was .300.

During another game with the Red Sox, the crack of Henry's bat reached Boston's dugout. Ted Williams, the Red Sox star slugger, asked, "Who hit that one?"

"Aaron, a new kid," a sportswriter told him.

"He sounds like quite a hitter," Williams said.

34

On the day before the regular season opened, Henry was called into the office of John Quinn, the Milwaukee Braves' general manager.

"You've had a great spring, Henry," Quinn told him. "So this probably won't surprise you." He handed Henry a Braves contract.

Henry was still only 20 years old. He had made the majors! As a Milwaukee regular he would be earning $8,000 a year.

Jim Bruton, oldest of the Braves' several black players, helped Henry feel at home with his new team. As their train pulled into the Braves' hometown for the first time, Bruton asked, "Where are you going, Henry?"

"Where the team wants me to stay, I guess," Henry said. He didn't know where that was. He had never been in Milwaukee before. And he was alone.

Barbara would not join him for some time.

"You come on home and have dinner with Loretta and me tonight," Bruton said. "We'll get you settled down later."

The Braves opened in Cincinnati. Henry went 0 for 4, and the Braves lost, 9-8. Neither Henry Aaron nor the Braves did much better during the next few weeks.

On April 23 the Braves started a series with the Cardinals. Henry went to bat seven times in the fourteen-inning game. The Cards' pitcher was the powerful Vic Raschi. Twice Henry got singles. In the fourth inning he drove out a home run, and the Braves won, 7-5.

Although no one realized it then, April 23, 1954, would go down in the record books. That was the day Henry Aaron started a long string of major-league homers that would guarantee him a place in the Baseball Hall of Fame.

Rookie Henry Aaron is congratulated by Charlie Grimm as he heads for the plate after a home run.

Two days later Henry clouted his second homer and got four singles as well.

His hitting wasn't always that good. He could hit to right, now, but pitchers could see that he had trouble with curve balls. They threw him curves all the time. Two of the Braves' best pitchers worked out with Henry for hours, and slowly he learned to connect with curves.

Henry had one other serious fault. He

was too ready to swing at anything. He had to work by himself to cure that one.

"I disciplined myself to wait for the good pitch," he said later.

The Braves' new rookie made other kinds of mistakes. Sometimes he threw a ball to the wrong base. And once he barely made it to third base when he should have scored. He had stopped to pick up his cap when it blew off.

But he was learning. One coach said, "He doesn't make the same mistake twice."

For a while the Braves' coaches wanted to change the way Henry ran, stiff-legged on his heels. He looked so slow and lazy they were afraid he would miss a lot of catches. But Henry usually caught the ball he chased, so they let him go on running in his own way.

One day Don Davidson, who handled the Braves' publicity, asked some sports-writers a question. "Why don't you ever write a story about Number 5, Henry Aaron?"

"He doesn't give us any good, lively stuff about himself," one of the writers told Davidson. "I ask him a question and Henry answers in one word."

"He makes some great plays," another said. "I've seen him make remarkable catches. I've seen him steal lots of bases. And he really can slam that ball. But he makes everything look so easy that nothing seems worth writing about."

"Why not call him Hank instead of Henry?" Davidson suggested. "That might make him sound more exciting."

The writers did as Davidson asked. Some of them even began to call Henry "Hammerin' Hank." But they still didn't write about him very often.

It was Don Davidson who had given Henry his uniform number. Henry somehow didn't like the number 5.

"Could I have a double number instead?" he asked Davidson. "A real double—like 22 or 55?"

Davidson looked closely at Henry's five-
foot-eleven figure. It was still thin. "I'm
not sure there's room for two numbers
on your back, Henry," he said. "But I'll
see about it."

All that season the Braves' fortunes
went up and down. Each time they got
close to first place, they dropped back
again. Henry heard people say, "They

Aaron scored the winning run in this 1954
game against the New York Giants.

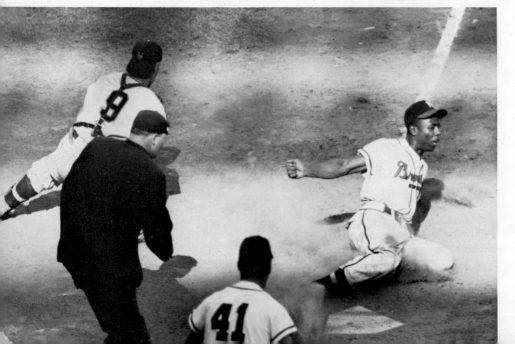

lost the pennant the day Thomson got hurt."

Henry kept feeling he ought to be doing more for the team, especially since he was taking Thomson's place. Every day he tried to improve his playing.

Two days before Labor Day the Braves played a doubleheader against Cincinnati. Henry came into the first game late and got a two-bagger his only time at bat. In the second game he got four for four.

His fourth hit came in the eighth inning. It was a screamer into center field. He was sliding into third when his foot caught in the bag. He couldn't get up.

At the hospital a doctor said, "The ankle is broken. We'll have to operate."

Resting in bed after the operation, Henry had plenty of time to think. Bobby Thomson's broken ankle had given him his chance. It was now healed, and Thomson was back in his old position.

Henry knew his own broken ankle might not heal that well. He knew the Braves might no longer need him. His first year with the majors might be his last.

He wished he had made a better record. He had hit .400 with the Clowns and .340 or more in the minors. As a major-leaguer he had hit .280, and the Braves had ended the season in third place.

But the Milwaukee sportswriters thought rookie Aaron's record was fine, even if he wasn't an exciting player. In his 122 games he had had 131 hits, 13 of them homers. He had driven in 69 runs. They unanimously voted him the Braves' Most Valuable Player of the Year.

If he could play again, Henry told himself, he would do his best to live up to that honor.

6. Number 44

Henry and Barbara spent the winter back in Mobile. He rested and played with his new baby daughter, Gaile. He was very proud of her.

By spring Henry's ankle seemed perfectly healed. The Braves did want him back, as a right fielder. And the uniform waiting for him now carried the number 44. Along with several other fielders, he went to Florida a week early for 1955 spring practice.

A baseball rule permitted only pitchers and catchers to report early. Baseball Commissioner Ford Frick sent telegrams which said the fielders would be fined.

Manager Charlie Grimm handed Henry his telegram. "It's from Ford Frick," he said.

Henry didn't understand Frick's name, the way Grimm said it. He thought Grimm was talking about some stranger.

"Who's he?" Henry asked.

Grimm told the sportswriters what Henry had said, and they finally had a good story about him. The next day fans all over the country were laughing at it.

"Imagine a ballplayer so green that he doesn't know who Frick is!" they said.

Reporters soon had a few other stories about Henry too. One was about a catcher telling Henry, "You're holding the bat wrong, kid. You're supposed to hold it so you can read the label."

Henry's answer was, "I came here to bat, not to read."

One of Henry's short answers led to another story. A writer, trying to learn

Aaron and teammates (left to right) Bobby Thomson, Gene Conley, and Davy O'Connell share a moment of victory.

the "secrets" of his hitting ability, asked Henry, "What do you look for when you come up to the plate?"

"The baseball," Henry told him.

Henry knew that some of these stories made the fans laugh at him. Still, he didn't complain because he knew publicity helped the team by bringing fans to the ball park.

The Braves were having a rough season. Injuries had sidelined some of their best pitchers and hitters. But Henry was playing great baseball.

He was picked for the All-Star Game, and he got two singles in his two times at bat. By July his average was up to .325. And though he was trying for base hits, he already had 22 homers.

Many people thought Henry looked half-asleep in the dugout. Opposing pitchers knew better. They knew he was studying every move they made—checking every pitch, judging their control. He was so tough to pitch to that they began calling him Bad Henry.

Don Newcombe, the Dodger pitching star, was asked how he would like to play Henry. "I wish I could throw the ball *under* the plate," he said.

And Tug McGraw of the Mets once said, "The way to pitch to Henry is the same way as to pitch to anybody else, except don't let the ball go."

The Braves ended their season in second place, thirteen and one-half games behind the Dodgers. Henry's own season ended with an average of .314. He had scored 105 runs, driven in another 106, and homered 27 times. Again he was named the team's Most Valuable Player.

The next spring the team was in fine shape. Henry was batting like a house afire. Everybody was hopeful. "This season we'll take the pennant!" the Braves said.

In May the team was in first place. Henry's average was .400!

Then the streak ended. By mid-June the Braves had dropped down to fifth spot. In one sixteen-game stretch, Henry got only a dozen hits.

All the players had heard rumors that Charlie Grimm would be fired if they didn't have a good year. Suddenly the rumors proved true. Tough Fred Haney

Henry Aaron is safe
at home for another
score and (left) re-
ceives a silver bat
as the 1956 batting
champion.

was brought in to replace Grimm. The new manager worked the Braves hard.

And Haney got results. The Braves shot back up to first place.

Except for one bad slump in August, Henry's bat was finding the ball again. Finally only one man stood between him and the batting championship—Wally Moon of the St. Louis Cardinals. Then Henry had three homers and two doubles in a Labor Day doubleheader against the Reds. Those hits put him ahead of Moon.

With only three games left on their schedule, the first-place Braves were one full game ahead of the Dodgers. Milwaukee really had pennant fever.

Then the Braves lost, and the Dodgers were rained out. The Braves' lead was cut to half a game.

The next day the Dodgers got two wins and went half a game ahead.

Every Brave and every Milwaukee fan knew the Braves had to win both of their last two games to stay in the race.

The first of those two games, against St. Louis, went to twelve innings. Henry got three of his team's eight hits—and won the batting championship with an average of .328. But the Braves lost, 2-1. With that loss went their chance for the pennant.

Henry led the league in doubles that year, with 34. He led it in hits, with 200. He led it in total bases, with 340. He hit 26 home runs.

But his team had gone down in defeat, and that was what counted most with him.

"For the first time in my life in the big leagues," he said, "I really knew what hurt was."

7. His "Shiningest Hour"

After a long, hard work-out the next spring, Henry said the Braves were "slim, trim, hungry, and ready to play." Many experts felt they had a real chance at the pennant.

Henry had his own private goals for 1957. He said, "I'd like to hit .345, hit 35 home runs, and bat in at least 100 runs."

The Braves started off like champions. They won nine of their first ten games. But four other clubs were also strong pennant contenders: the Dodgers, the Reds, the Phillies, and the Cardinals. It was a close race from the start.

Manager Haney didn't think of Henry as a slugger, but as a dependable hitter. So he put him second in the batting order. This meant Henry could often score, as sluggers Joe Adcock and Ed Mathews followed him to the plate.

Henry himself said, "I just want to be known as a singles hitter." But he did like to drive in runs, and batting second gave him little chance to do that. As usual, he didn't complain. Instead he just slammed balls all over the field.

The famous Bobby Thomson, on the other hand, wasn't doing so well at bat. Haney soon traded him for second baseman Red Schoendienst, a good switch hitter. And when Red entered the batting order, Henry was shifted to the fourth spot, after Mathews.

Henry liked the change. The fans loved it. Henry and Mathews proved to be a deadly pair of hitting teammates.

Mathews and Aaron held slots three and four in the batting order and together set new slugging records.

On June 15 the Braves were in first place in the tight race. Then injuries knocked out first baseman Adcock and center fielder Joe Bruton. Haney had to make some shifts. He moved Henry to center field to support two new outfielders from the minors.

Henry had been leading the league in batting, in home runs, and in RBIs (runs batted in). But the strain of playing in the new position sent his averages down, and that affected the team.

"It's a little unfair to Henry," one Milwaukee sportswriter wrote, "but . . . when he isn't swishing that bat with authority, the Braves are in trouble."

By now opposing pitchers were also telling Henry, in their own way, how important he was. They were brushing him back with close pitches and forcing him to hit the dirt with even closer ones.

One day Henry slammed a double off the fence, against Giant pitcher Johnny Antonelli. The pitcher wanted to get even. The next time Henry came up, Antonelli called out, "You can afford to lose some teeth!"

"But can you?" Henry called back.

Antonelli smoked a chin-high fastball at him. Henry stepped back and swung. The ball landed in the upper stands, some 450 feet from home plate.

Antonelli and the other pitchers soon learned that Henry didn't scare easily.

In August the Braves went on a winning streak that put them eight games ahead of the second-place Cardinals. By early September the pennant seemed secure.

Then came a slump. The Braves lost eight games out of eleven, while the Cards won ten out of twelve. The Braves' lead dropped to two and one-half games.

But Henry's hitting was holding up. He had already passed his goal of 35 homers for the season. Henry hit his 40th on September 10, his 41st a week later.

The Braves were pulling back up by then. On September 22, when Henry drove out homer number 42, the Braves beat the Cubs in a twelve-inning game. One more victory now would give them the pennant. They had to win it from the Cards.

Over 40,000 excited fans jammed the Milwaukee stadium on the big night. The score was 2-2 at the end of the ninth.

Neither team scored in the tenth. The Cardinals failed again in their half of the eleventh.

When Henry came up to bat in the Braves' half of that inning, two men were out and there was a man on base. A solid hit could mean a run, the game, and the pennant. The fans were on their feet.

"Out of the park, Hank!" they yelled. "Slam it!"

Aaron is carried off the field following his pennant-winning home run.

Henry faced the Cardinals' pitcher. The ball zoomed toward him. He swung.

The ball sailed over the center-field fence. And the fans went wild. The pennant was theirs!

Six years earlier seventeen-year-old Henry Aaron had raced along a Mobile street, pretending he was Bobby Thomson scoring his pennant-winning run. Now Henry had his own triumph. As his teammates carried him off the field, he knew that this was, as he later said, his "shiningest hour."

He capped it the next day in the season's last game. In the first inning, with the bases full, he clouted his 44th home run of the year—his first grand slam. He was ready to face the New York Yankees in the World Series.

The powerful Yankees had been picked to win—and they did win the first game, 3-1. Henry had a single in the fourth inning, but he struck out in the sixth, leaving two men on base.

He did better the next day. So did the rest of the Braves. Henry hit a triple and came home to score. Milwaukee won, 4-2.

The third game was a slaughter. The Yanks took it, 12-3.

The fourth game seesawed from inning to inning. Henry's homer in the fourth, with two men on, put the Braves ahead. The Yankees tied them in the ninth. Mathews's homer in the tenth gave the Braves a hard-won 7-5 victory.

The Braves won the fifth game too, 1-0. Henry's sixth-inning hit had put Mathews in scoring position for that one run. Milwaukee was now ahead in the Series, three games to two.

Then the Yankees tied up the Series by winning 3-2, in spite of Henry's seventh-inning homer.

On the day of the seventh and deciding game, the Braves came into New York's Yankee Stadium ready to fight to the death. They didn't have to fight that hard. An easy 5-0 win gave them the World Series. Milwaukee had its first baseball championship!

More than 20,000 fans waited at the Milwaukee airport for the team's return. Almost 500,000 lined the route of the five-mile victory parade. There was dancing in the streets. Bells rang. Whistles blew.

Milwaukee's great year had also been a great one for Henry Aaron. His fielding, a sportswriter said, had been "flawless." His World Series batting average had been .393, with three homers and seven RBIs. Henry had averaged .322 for the season, not far below his goal. He had led the league in runs scored, with 118; in total bases, with 369; and in runs

Henry Aaron was everywhere
in the 1957 World Series—

slugging out home runs. . .

making stops in the outfield. . .

crossing home plate to the cheers of his teammates.

batted in, with 132—32 more than he had hoped for. And he had homered 44 times.

The Baseball Writers Association paid him the highest honor it could bestow. It named him the National League's Most Valuable Player.

Henry had already bought a comfortable home in a Milwaukee suburb for Barbara and their two children. Little Gaile was now four. Henry, Jr., had been born the previous spring. A third baby was expected. Henry knew his new importance had earned him a big raise. He could afford to settle down and enjoy the winter in the way he liked best, at home with his family.

8. After the Championship

That winter brought unexpected sorrow to the Aarons. Barbara gave birth to twin boys, and one of them soon died. When Henry reported for 1958 spring training, he was still grieving over the baby's death.

Back in right field again that season, he started off so badly that his June election to the All-Star Game surprised him.

The election also snapped him out of his slump. He went on a hitting streak and carried the Braves along with him. They moved steadily up toward first place. Henry was earning a .326 average for the season. He was going to win the

Golden Glove as the league's best defensive right fielder. And the Braves were heading for another pennant.

They won it on September 21, in a clinching game with Cincinnati. Henry's two-run double and two-run homer had given them a 6-5 victory.

The fans were jubilant. Their team had made it to the World Series for the second year in a row. This time, too, the Braves would fight the Yankees for the title, and they expected another win.

After the first four games, that win looked certain. The Braves had taken three of those contests. No team had lost a World Series with that kind of a start for more than 30 years.

But the Yankees didn't give up. They wanted revenge for their 1957 defeat. They took it in the next three games: 7-0, 4-3, and 6-2. The stunned Braves had lost the world championship!

That began a long downward slide for the Braves. They made the division playoffs in 1959. But by 1963 they had dropped to sixth place.

Older team members were traded away. New men were brought in. One of them was Henry's young brother, Tommie, up from the minors. Nothing helped.

Henry's own records were holding up. In 1959 he had won another Golden Glove and another batting championship. His average had been .355 and he had hit 39 home runs.

In most of the following years he led the league in one or more departments. In 1963 he led in RBIs, in runs scored, and in total bases. He was hitting a lot of homers too—45 in 1962; 44 in 1963.

He and Ed Mathews together were also piling up a remarkable two-man record. By 1965 they had batted out 863 home runs between them. They had

Aaron (44) and Mathews (41) walk up the ramp in Milwaukee for the last time.

topped the record of 793 set years before by the great Yankee slugging team of Lou Gehrig and Babe Ruth.

But the Milwaukee fans had lost interest in their losing team. For some time there had been talk of moving the Braves to another city. Henry hoped that wouldn't happen.

But the players had nothing to say about the decision. When they finished the 1965 season, they knew it was their last in Milwaukee. Next year they would become the Braves of Atlanta, Georgia.

9. The Braves of Atlanta

Fans by the hundred thousands cheered the motorcade that welcomed the Braves to Atlanta. The Georgia city was just as enthusiastic about its new team as Milwaukee had been thirteen years before, when the Braves arrived there from Boston. Henry's car could barely move through the excited crowds.

Henry knew what Atlantans hoped to see when they came to their new stadium. "If I didn't hit a lot of home runs," Henry once explained, "I'd be a flop. . . ."

The fans saw their first Aaron four-bagger on April 29, and their second three days later. Henry's total of 44 for that 1966 season led the league. /

He also led the league that year in RBIs, and he set a record by stealing 21 bases in 24 attempts. But his .279 batting average was Henry's lowest yet. Swinging for home runs, he once said, ". . . cost me."

The Braves spent the season near the bottom of the Western Division. Nevertheless a million and a half Atlantans had come out to watch them play. And the Aaron family already felt comfortably settled in their new home.

That winter Ed Mathews was traded, leaving Henry as the team's undisputed top man. A raise to $100,000 finally gave him a superstar's salary.

In other ways, however, 1967 was almost a replay of 1966. Batting at a .500 rate early in June, Henry drove out four homers in four days. During that slugging streak he also got his eleventh grand slam. His 39 homers led the league again. But the Braves ended up in seventh place, 24½ games behind the winning Cardinals.

By July of the following year, Henry Aaron was nearing the 500th home run of his career. His homers numbers 498 and 499 both came on July 7. A trophy with the number 500 on it in gold was ready before his next game. His father came from Mobile for the event.

Henry didn't hit a home run that day. He didn't homer in the next two games either. Then Mr. Aaron had to go home.

"You'll probably get it today, son," he said before he left.

And Henry did. On July 14, 1968, playing against San Francisco, Henry got hold of a fast ball. He sent it 400 feet over the center-field fence.

The team was waiting for him at home plate. William Bartholomay, head of the Braves' management, presented the trophy. The fans cheered him. Henry had become the eighth man in major-league history to hit 500 or more home runs.

The Braves crawled up to fifth place that year. Henry's own records for the season showed a drop. His home-run total was only 29. His RBIs and runs had fallen off too. His average of .287 would have satisfied most players. But it didn't satisfy Henry.

He had been feeling tired from time to time. Late in the season he had even agreed to try first base. He thought it might be easier on his legs than chasing balls in the outfield.

The first-base experiment didn't continue into 1969. The team had acquired a seasoned first baseman in Orlando Cepeda. Henry was back in the outfield, operating with his usual quiet efficiency.

He had been named the team's captain, and he enjoyed helping the younger players make progress.

The whole team made progress that year. It won the Western Division title. But in spite of Henry's three homers, one in each of three games, the Braves lost the play-off series against the "Miracle" Mets.

Henry had been a kingpin in most of the season's victories. He had also passed some new milestones. His June 2 homer, number 522, took him past the record of Boston slugger Ted Williams. His number 525 on June 24 beat Jimmy Foxx's record. On July 30 his number 537 carried him past Mickey Mantle into third place in the all-time home-run standings. Now only Willie Mays and the great Babe Ruth had hit more homers than Hammerin' Hank Aaron.

By the end of 1969, only two men stood
between Aaron and history: Willie Mays
(above) and Babe Ruth, with 714 homers.

For the fourth time in his career, Henry's homers that year had totaled 44, the number he wore. "What would have happened," a Braves official wondered, "if we'd given him uniform number 77?"

The number 44 was still in Henry's mind when the 1970 season started. He needed only 44 more hits to reach a total of 3,000. When he did that, he would join a "club" of only eight men. Its only living member then was Stan Musial.

As the Braves started a doubleheader against Cincinnati on May 17, Henry had 2,999 hits to his credit.

In the first game Henry grounded out twice, flied out once, and struck out.

The suspense ended in the second game's first inning. Henry hit an infield grounder to the shortstop, and he got to first before the throw could be made.

Stan Musial was one of the first to congratulate him.

Later that season Henry could congratulate Willie Mays when Mays became the club's third living member.

Henry ended the season with an average of .298, 118 RBIs, and 38 home runs. The last homer was number 592. Willie Mays was still ahead of him, with 628, but Henry was narrowing the gap.

Henry was proud of his 3,000 hits. "To make 3,000 base hits, you have to be mighty consistent," he said.

But now there was another goal in view. Thirty-six-year-old Henry talked about it at the end of the 1970 season.

"People keep wanting to know if I will be around long enough to break Ruth's home-run record," he said. "I don't know. I do know I will not hang around just for the sake of hanging on, picking up twelve one year, maybe twenty the next. I have too much respect for baseball to do that."

10. Chasing the Babe

Early in 1971 Henry and his wife were divorced. They had married very young, and over the years both of them had changed. Henry talked about it very little. He simply worked harder than ever.

Once more the Braves needed a man on first, and Henry was shifted there for some 70 games. He batted .327, drove in 118 runs, and homered 47 times, his all-time high. Henry even homered in the All-Star Game, after hitting only singles in his sixteen earlier games.

On April 27, 1971, Henry hit his 600th home run. And reporters now talked more often about that magic number 714.

"Do you think you'll catch the Babe?" they asked.

"That's still a long way off," Henry always answered.

By the season's end his home runs numbered 639, only seven behind Willie Mays's 646—and Mays was already 40 years old.

"If any player living today reaches the Babe's record, that player has got to be Henry Aaron," sportswriters were saying.

The Braves' owner thought that Henry's growing home-run total would win new fans. And by 1972 the Braves needed some, after finishing third in 1971. So Henry was given a new $200,000-a-year contract that made him baseball's highest-paid player. The contract was for three years.

Henry wasn't sure he would play three more years. He was tired more often now, especially when a game followed a long plane trip. A knee injury was giving him trouble. He wasn't sleeping well. All these things hurt his playing. His hits no longer came so regularly. He was making fielding errors.

"Looks like he's over the hill," the manager said. He talked of trading Henry for someone younger.

Bartholomay was determined to keep Henry. He replaced the manager with Henry's old teammate and batting partner, Eddie Mathews.

Aaron covers first base in a game against the Chicago Cubs.

Mathews went to see Henry. "Wouldn't you be happier back in right field?" he asked.

"I sure would!" Henry told him.

Soon afterward Henry decided he still wasn't doing a good job.

"The ball leaves my hand as fast as ever," he said, "but it travels slower and dies sooner. Base runners are taking advantage of me. I'm hurting the club."

Mathews shifted him to left field. For a time that seemed to help. But all the Braves knew Henry was having a bad time.

His fans knew it too. They loved him anyway. When he homered again, in that year's All-Star Game, they rose and applauded him so hard the stands shook.

The season ended as badly as it had begun. The Braves finished a poor fourth. Henry's .265 average was his lowest yet. He had batted in only 77 runs. But he homered 34 times to bring his total to 673 and and past Willie Mays.

Until 1972 many people had known almost nothing at all about Henry Aaron. His quiet style was one reason for that. Another was the Braves' low ratings recently. Those ratings had kept the team from being much noticed outside its own division. Now everybody wanted to learn about the Brave who might someday break Ruth's record—the record experts had said would never be broken.

At the opening of the 1973 season, Henry's teammates gave him a cake for his 39th birthday. The lettering on it said:

Happy Birthday, Hank
39 and 41 to go

"And you'll knock out those 41 more homers," the other players told him. "It's just a matter of time."

In April 1973 Henry got only eight hits. Five of them were home runs. On May 1 he slammed out two circuit clouts. On May 13 he got one home run in each game of a doubleheader. Every week from then on Henry got at least one more homer. On July 20 his total was 699.

The next night the left-field stands of the Atlanta stadium were jammed. The Braves had offered 700 silver dollars to the retriever of Henry's number 700 ball. The fans in the left-field stands thought they had the best chance to catch it.

The big moment came in the third inning, on Henry's second time at bat. He sent the ball straight into the left-field stands. An eighteen-year-old student caught it. Afterward, in the clubhouse, the student offered his reward to Henry's favorite charity.

Henry smiled at him. "No, you keep it," he said.

Then he patiently answered the reporters' questions while cameras clicked and buzzed around him.

The one thing reporters knew they shouldn't ask him about was his children. He wanted to keep their lives as private as possible. His two sons were spending the summer with him. To them Henry was a father, not a famous man. Usually he got up early and drove Larry to his summer-school classes. Later, after cooking his own breakfast, he often stopped to buy a take-out lunch on his way to the ball park. This was for Hank, Jr., who worked with the Braves' ground crew.

One of the few people Henry could relax with, outside his own family, was his friend, Mrs. Billye Williams. She interviewed well-known people for an Atlanta television station, and Henry had appeared on her program.

Mrs. Williams was the widow of a Baptist minister who had worked with Martin Luther King, Jr. She too was active in the civil rights movement. Henry was speaking out more often now about blacks' needs for equal rights and opportunities, and she encouraged him.

By mid-summer of 1973 Henry's new fame was bringing him thousands of letters. Some of them disturbed him.

"Everybody loved Babe Ruth," one letter said. "You will be the most hated guy in this country and elsewhere if you break his record."

Many letter writers seemed especially angry because Henry might break the record of a white man. Some letters were so ugly and threatening that the Braves arranged to have Henry guarded.

Reporters learned about those letters and told the public about them. Thousands of Americans immediately wrote to

Henry to let him know they were behind him.

Young people, especially, said that they
hoped he would break the home-run record. To many of them Babe Ruth seemed
a part of ancient history. They wanted a
new home-run king, a hero for their own
generation.

And a congressman said in a speech,
"I am sure that if Babe Ruth were alive
today he would be saying, 'Right on,
Hank,' just as millions of other Americans, white and black, are saying. . . ."

In the Braves' hometown, the Chamber
of Commerce started a campaign called
"Atlanta Salutes Henry Aaron." Large
billboards carried Henry's picture and the
number of his latest homer. Clubs honored him with gifts and banquets. A
Henry Aaron Scholarship Fund was es-
tablished for needy high-school students.

The excitement increased as the season

wore on. By September 10, the day that Henry batted out his 710th homer, television cameramen were surrounding him wherever he went. Radios were blaring out songs called "Move Over, Babe" and "Hammerin' Henry." Reporters asked pitchers how they would feel if they gave up the pitch that tied the Babe's record. A Pittsburgh Pirate pitcher wrote his own song in answer to that question. Some of its words were:

Please!
I've got a reputation
And I've got a fam-il-y.
So please don't hit it
So please don't hit it
So please don't hit it off of me.

Number 711 came on September 17. Number 712 came five days later. Then a week went by without one.

On September 29, the next-to-the-last day of the season, the Braves played the Houston Astros. When the Astro pitcher walked Henry on his first time at bat, the fans booed.

In the third inning Henry came up again and swung at the first pitch. As the ball sailed over the left-field fence, the cheering crowd rose to its feet. Henry had hit his 713th! One more would tie the record.

The cheering went on for so long that Henry had to come out of the dugout and tip his hat to end it.

Lines formed at the box office early the next morning. More than 40,000 fans were on hand for the season's last game. Rain began to drizzle down. The crowd ignored it.

Henry drove in a run his first time up. He got a single the second time. On his third time up he had another single.

And the home runs
keep on coming!

Number 640—April 22, 1972

Number 648—May 31, 1972

Number 693—June 29, 1973

Number 700—July 21, 1973

Then Henry came up to the plate for the last time—and popped out!

As he jogged away across the muddy field, the crowd was on its feet again. Louder and louder their cheering voices rose.

Henry tipped his cap to the stands. Still the cheering went on. A sportswriter called it "the most moving ovation I'd ever seen for any man."

The season was over. Thirty-nine-year-old Henry Aaron had batted .301. He had driven in 96 runs. He had homered 40 times. He had come within one home run of the record.

But that night, when reporters asked him how he felt, it was the fans Henry was thinking of. "I'm sorry I couldn't hit one for them, sitting in the rain and all," he said.

11. A New Home-Run King

In November 1973 Henry Aaron and Mrs. Billye Williams were married. Henry's four children were all doing well. He had signed a contract to help advertise the products of a television set manufacturer. It made him a millionaire. Henry Aaron knew he was a lucky man.

He also knew he still had a job to do on the ball field. He couldn't relax until it was done. And it would have to be done under especially difficult conditions. The pressure on him was enormous.

All during spring training, hundreds of people wanted to talk to him, to get his autograph. Writers and photographers followed him everywhere.

Thousands of dollars were being offered for the balls with which Henry would tie and break Ruth's record. But most people thought those historic baseballs should go to the Baseball Hall of Fame Museum. To make sure the right ones got there, special balls were being prepared. Until Henry tied the record, each ball pitched to him would be marked 714, in invisible ink. After that the balls would be marked 715.

April 4, 1974, opening day, finally arrived. Cheers greeted Henry's arrival on the field in Cincinnati. Just ten minutes later the stands were roaring. Cincinnati's Jack Billingham had pitched a marked ball to Henry, and Henry had slammed it over the fence. Babe Ruth's record was tied!

"Can you imagine that?" Manager Ed

Mathews was saying. "His first time up, his first swing at the ball, and he hits it out!"

A policeman stationed behind the left-field fence retrieved the ball, and it was given to Henry.

"I'd certainly like to thank you very much," Henry said quietly into the microphone brought out on the field. "I'm just glad it's almost over with."

Long minutes went by before the game could get underway again.

Henry grounded to third his next time up. He was walked in the fifth, and he lined out to center in the seventh. The Braves lost, 6–7.

Afterward, in the dugout, Henry refused the champagne the Braves' management had bought for his celebration. He never felt like celebrating when his team had lost.

Henry went hitless in his second game

with Cincinnati. And then the Braves went home.

Atlanta's welcoming ceremony for Henry took place on the evening of April 8, before 53,775 fans. Henry's wife and parents watched from a special stadium box. His brother Tommie couldn't be there. He was managing a Braves' farm team in Savannah. But Charlie Grimm, who had given Henry his chance with the Braves, was an honored guest. So was Ed Scott, who had persuaded Henry's mother to let her fifteen-year-old son join the Mobile Black Bears.

A great map of the United States had been painted on the outfield grass. It showed the cities where Henry had hit his milestone homers. Balloons were floating through the misty twilight. A band marched and played. A choir sang. The mayor of Atlanta and the governor of Georgia made speeches. There were gifts for Henry. And always there was the joyful roar of the crowd.

"Thank you. Thank you very much," Henry said.

Then Henry's father threw out the first ball and the game began.

Henry came up to bat for the first time in the second inning. Al Downing, the Dodger pitcher, threw him one strike and four balls. The fans booed and Henry walked to first.

A few minutes later, on a double hit by Dusty Baker, Henry scored for the 2,063rd time in his career. That broke a National League record Willie Mays had held until that moment.

It was raining when Henry came up again in the fourth. Downing sent him one ball. Then Downing wound up and threw again. For the first time that evening, Henry's powerful wrists flicked the bat forward. Wood met leather.

**Henry Aaron sends home run number 715
up, up, and away over the wall.**

As the fans came to their feet, the ball rose high toward left centerfield. The Dodger left fielder raced after it. He climbed the fence—but the ball disappeared over it.

And now the crowd went wild. As skyrockets flared into the night, the scoreboard flashed the number 715.

Babe Ruth's record had been broken. The next day's headlines would say simply HENRY DOES IT.

Henry trotted home to his waiting teammates while 35,000,000 people watched him on their television screens. Henry's mother and father were on the field, and they hugged him. He pushed through the crowd to kiss his wife.

Then Henry held up the number 715 ball. It had been caught by Tom House, a young Braves bullpenner. And the fans went on roaring.

When the ballgame finally started up

again, Al Downing seemed shaken. The crowd cheered him when he left the field. And the Braves won, 7–4.

—That night Henry did celebrate, first with his teammates, then at home with his family.

"I just thank God it's all over," Henry had said into the microphone during those long minutes of excitement on the field.

But of course it wasn't over yet. There was the All-Star Game, to which Henry was elected by the largest majority in National League history. He was honored in every city on the Braves' schedule. And by the season's end 18 more home runs had raised his record to 733!

Early in November Henry visited in Japan, where baseball is a favorite sport. He had been invited to meet Japan's greatest hitter, Sadaharu Oh, in a home-run contest. Fifty thousand fans jammed the big Tokyo stadium for the event.

94

Henry Aaron,
new home-run king.

Television carried it to audiences on both sides of the world.

Each man received twenty pitches. The Japanese star turned nine of his into homers. Henry won the contest by sending ten balls out of the park!

That same day the world learned that Henry Aaron would not retire from baseball, as had been expected. The Braves had asked him to join their office staff. They wanted him to travel around making speeches about the team. Henry wasn't interested in that kind of a job. But he had decided he still wasn't ready to leave the game that had been his whole life. He signed a contract with the Milwaukee Brewers of the American League.

"I'm going back to Milwaukee, to the city where I started my career," he told reporters with a happy grin. "I'm going back home."

Milwaukee welcomed him with open arms. Every town in America would have welcomed Henry Aaron just as enthusiastically. He had earned the title of the new home-run king, but he was still the modest, hard-working ballplayer millions of fans had learned to love.

When the new contract was announced, many people said the same thing that had been said about Henry Aaron when he slammed home his historic number 714. They said, "It couldn't have happened to a better man, a finer gentleman."

THE BASEBALL FIELD

The baseball field is made up of the "diamond," the infield and the outfield.

The diamond is actually a 90-foot square with a base in each corner. This basic plan for the diamond was first written in the rules of the game in 1845.

The bases are white canvas bags, 15 inches square and 3 to 5 inches thick. Home base is a 17-inch square with two of the corners cut off. This five-sided slab of white rubber is level with the ground surface.

The batter stands in a box 4 feet wide and 6 feet long. The pitcher throws from a mound that is 10 inches higher than the level of the base line.

The distance from home base to the nearest outfield fence must be at least 250 feet. The backstop is 60 feet behind the home base. The players' benches must be at least 25 feet from the nearest base line. These benches are in the dugouts.

A Little League diamond is ⅔ the size of the regulation playing field.

right fielder ●

OUTFIELD

● center fielder

OUTFIELD

● left fielder